# ARMY

## Civilian to SOLDIER

by Meish Goldish

Consultant: Fred Pushies
U.S. SOF Adviser

# BEARPORT
PUBLISHING

New York, New York

**Credits**

**Cover and Title Page,** © Andrew A. Nelles/ZUMA Press/Newscom and U.S. Army/Sgt. Matthew Moeller; 4, © Craig F. Walker/The Denver Post/ZUMA Press/Newscom; 5, © Craig F. Walker/The Denver Post/ZUMA Press/Newscom; 6, © Craig F. Walker/The Denver Post/ZUMA Press/Newscom; 7, © Craig F. Walker/The Denver Post/ZUMA Press/Newscom; 8, © Craig F. Walker/The Denver Post; 9, © Craig F. Walker/The Denver Post; 10, © Jessica Rinaldi/Reuters/Landov; 11, © Craig F. Walker/The Denver Post/ZUMA Press/Newscom; 12, © Scott Olson/Getty Images; 13T, © U.S. Air Force photo/Staff Sgt. Larry A. Simmons; 13B, © Scott Olson/Getty Images; 14, © Susanne Kappler/Fort Jackson Leader; 15T, © Susanne Kappler/Fort Jackson Leader; 15B, © Caroline Gotler/The Bayonet; 16, © Tim Dominick/The State/MCT/Landov; 17, © Tim Dominick/The State/MCT/Newscom; 18, © U.S. Army photo/Mr. Carlton Wallace; 19, © Craig F. Walker/The Denver Post/ZUMA Press/Newscom; 20, © U.S. Air Force photo/Senior Airman Desiree N. Palacios; 21, © Craig F. Walker/The Denver Post/ZUMA Press/Newscom; 22, © Robin Trimarchi/Columbus Ledger-Enquirer/Newscom.

Publisher: Kenn Goin
Senior Editor: Lisa Wiseman
Creative Director: Spencer Brinker
Design: Debrah Kaiser
Photo Researcher: James O'Connor

*Library of Congress Cataloging-in-Publication Data*

Goldish, Meish.
  Army : civilian to soldier / by Meish Goldish.
    p. cm. — (Becoming a solider)
  Includes bibliographical references and index.
  ISBN-13: 978-1-936088-11-9 (library binding)
  ISBN-10: 1-936088-11-8 (library binding)
  1. Basic training (Military education) —United States—Juvenile literature.
  2. United States. Army—Military life—Juvenile literature. I. Title.
  U408.3.G64 2011
  355.5'40973—dc22
                        2010008026

For more information, write to Bearport Publishing Company, Inc., 101 Fifth Avenue, Suite 6R, New York, New York 10003. Printed in the United States of America in North Mankato, Minnesota.

062010
042110CGB

10 9 8 7 6 5 4 3 2 1

# Contents

# War Games

The **recruits** in the **platoon** quietly moved uphill, hiding behind bushes along the way. When they came to an enemy village, they heard machine-gun blasts inside a building. The men rushed toward the structure to search for the shooters. As more shots rang out, 18 members of the platoon fell to the ground. Had they been killed?

Recruit Ian Fisher hides behind some bushes—out of sight from the enemy.

Luckily, no one actually died because the attack wasn't real. It was an army training exercise. Yet for recruits such as Ian Fisher, the exercise showed that it takes skill and hard work to succeed as a soldier in the U.S. Army.

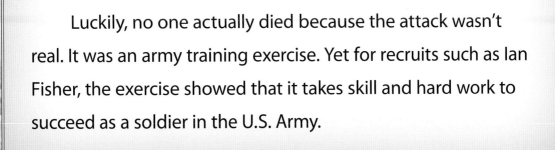

Ian and members of his platoon after hearing the machine-gun blasts

The army is the branch of the **armed forces** that is trained to fight on land.

# Signing Up

When Ian turned 17 years old in 2006, he announced to his family that he wanted to become a solider. At that time, the United States had already been at war with Iraq, a country in the Middle East, for a few years. Ian was eager to help out. "I love my country and want to fight for it," he said. So like thousands of other **patriotic** young men and women, Ian **enlisted** in the U.S. Army after finishing high school.

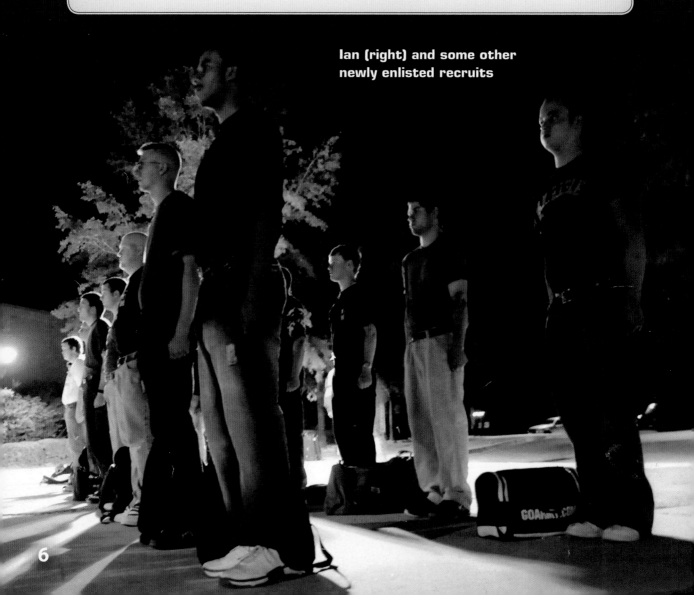

Ian (right) and some other newly enlisted recruits

Soon after, Ian was sent to Fort Benning, an army base in Georgia, for basic **combat** training, also known as BCT. This is a grueling nine-week program that all army recruits go through to learn combat skills as well as army history and values. It's during this time that **civilians** such as Ian become soldiers.

Before their basic training begins, army recruits spend a week in **orientation**. During this time, they receive their uniforms and equipment. Male recruits get very short haircuts or shave their heads, while females must make sure their hair is not longer than the collars of their uniforms.

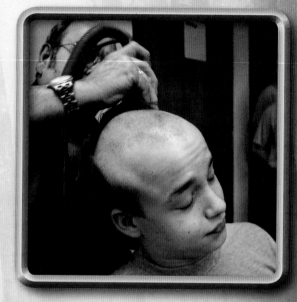

Ian Fisher closes his eyes as he gets a typical army haircut—a shaved head.

The U.S. Army has five locations where recruits can do their basic training: Fort Benning in Georgia, Fort Jackson in South Carolina, Fort Knox in Kentucky, Fort Leonard Wood in Missouri, and Fort Sill in Oklahoma.

U.S. Army Basic Combat Training Locations

# The Bag Drill

On their first day of training, nervous new arrivals find out just how tough the army can be. About 200 recruits are led outside. Their **duffel bags** lie in a tall pile. The group is given two minutes for each member to grab his or her bag and get back into line.

Recruits try to find their duffel bags in the giant pile.

The job is nearly impossible. In such a short amount of time, the confused recruits can't find their bags, which look exactly like all the other bags. If they don't succeed, the recruits are punished. For example, Ian Fisher and his group of fellow recruits had to hold their heavy bags over their heads as punishment. After trying again and again to find their bags, the recruits finally discover that the only way to succeed is by working together. To do that, a few people are chosen to call out the names that appear on each bag. The recruits can then claim their bags in a fast and orderly way.

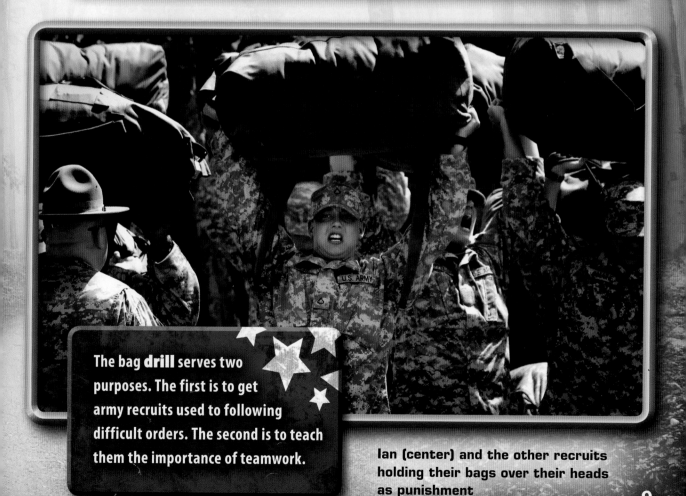

The bag **drill** serves two purposes. The first is to get army recruits used to following difficult orders. The second is to teach them the importance of teamwork.

Ian (center) and the other recruits holding their bags over their heads as punishment

# The Drill Sergeant

After the bag drill, recruits are divided into platoons, each of which has about 35 members. Platoons are then assigned **barracks** and a **drill sergeant**, who is in charge of the group for the next nine weeks.

A drill sergeant scolds one of his recruits inside the barracks. Each army platoon lives together in its own barracks, though men and women are grouped separately.

When speaking to a drill sergeant, recruits must address him or her as "Drill Sergeant." For example, a recruit answering yes would say, "Yes, Drill Sergeant!"

Drill sergeants are known for being tough. They will often stand directly in front of a recruit and yell orders. They also punish anyone who makes a mistake. For example, a recruit whose bed isn't made properly or who salutes the wrong way may be forced to do push-ups. "Drop and give me 20!" is a common order heard from a drill sergeant telling a recruit to do 20 push-ups.

**Ian Fisher performing push-ups as a punishment**

11

# Body Building

One of the drill sergeant's jobs is to get the platoon into top **physical** shape. Recruits wake up very early each day—at 4:30 A.M. They begin the day with physical training, which lasts for about an hour and a half. They start by running at a quick, steady pace. The drill sergeant yells at them to make sure everyone stays together at all times. Even when they are out of breath, the recruits must keep moving fast.

Recruits stretch before they begin their physical training.

Since recruits need to be physically fit in order to succeed as soldiers, more time is spent on physical exercise than any other kind of training during the nine weeks of BCT.

Though the recruits are tired after the run, there is no time to stop. Next, they are required to do dozens of push-ups and sit-ups. Then they finish their morning exercises with another run—an exhausting two-miles (3.2 km). Though their muscles ache, the recruits grow stronger and tougher week by week.

During physical training, recruits also do other exercises such as leg lifts.

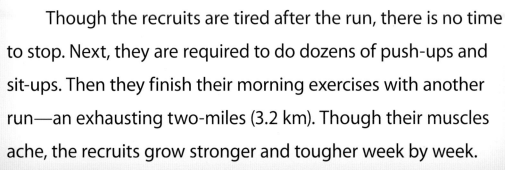

A female recruit doing push-ups

# Fighting Skills

Besides being physically fit, army soldiers must know how to fight. At times, their job will put them in contact with enemies and they need to know how to protect themselves.

During BCT, recruits are trained in hand-to-hand combat. This means that they learn how to kick, punch, and choke an enemy without using a **weapon**. Some of the skills they're taught are the same ones used in boxing and karate.

Recruits learn how to fight with their hands and feet in case they come face-to-face with an enemy.

Recruits are also trained to use dangerous combat weapons. They learn how to stab an enemy with the razor-sharp tip of a **bayonet**. They are taught how to toss a **grenade**, which will explode with deadly force within seconds after being thrown at a target. Their main weapon, however, is the M16 rifle. They often practice their rifle skills, which include assembling, shooting, and cleaning their weapons, for hours at a time.

Recruits spend more time on rifle practice than on any other part of their training, except for physical exercise.

Female recruits receive combat training, just as males do. However, U.S. law does not allow female soldiers to fight in army combat units. Instead, they perform jobs that help support other soldiers, such as flying helicopters and providing medical care to the injured.

Recruits also learn how to use a grenade launcher, which can launch a grenade a greater distance than a soldier can throw by hand.

# Over, Under, and Across

In a war, soldiers must be able to move about on any kind of battlefield, whether it is in a forest or in a mountainous area. Recruits prepare by training on an **obstacle course**. They learn to climb over tall walls without falling. They cross wobbly bridges made of shaky ropes or logs without plunging to the ground or water below. They crawl under sharp, barbed-wire fences without cutting themselves too badly. All these tasks take strength and concentration. One wrong move can lead to serious injury or even death.

Soldiers must make it across this part of the obstacle course by crawling along a rope.

While on the course, recruits must think of more than just themselves. They are taught to help fellow platoon members who have a hard time with any obstacle. Teamwork is a key part of army training.

Here, recruits use teamwork to help one another over a wall on the obstacle course.

After the first few weeks of BCT, each recruit is assigned a "battle buddy." For the rest of training, these two soldiers are responsible for each other at all times. If one of them wakes up late, for example, both buddies may be punished for it.

# The Final Test

In the eighth week of BCT, recruits face one big final test—a field training exercise. The platoon starts by marching six miles (9.7 km) in heat that can be more than 100°F (38°C). Each recruit must carry about 50 to 60 pounds (23 to 27 kg) of combat equipment along the way.

**An example of a field training exercise march**

Sweaty and tired after their march, the recruits enter the woods, where they must survive in a warlike setting. Fake gunfire and bombs go off all around them. They must move about the area safely, with only a map and **compass** to guide them. Anyone who makes a mistake on the battlefield can be declared "dead." Luckily for these recruits, it's only a fake war, and they can learn from their mistakes. In an actual battle, a careless soldier might pay for mistakes with his or her life.

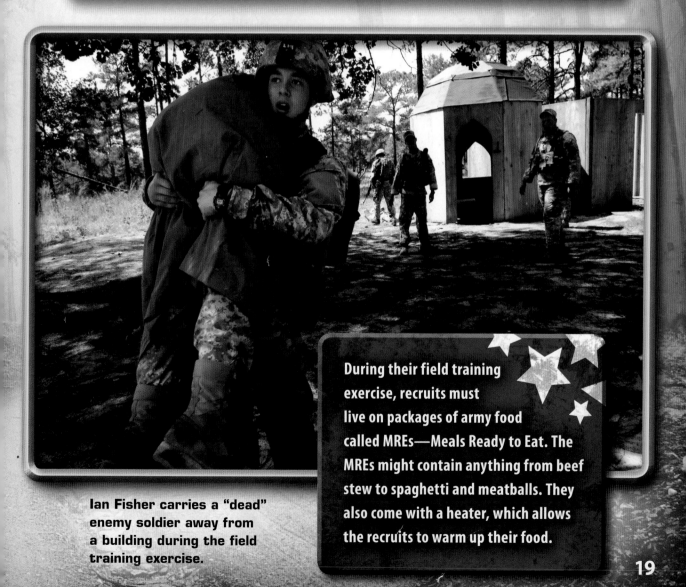

Ian Fisher carries a "dead" enemy soldier away from a building during the field training exercise.

During their field training exercise, recruits must live on packages of army food called MREs—Meals Ready to Eat. The MREs might contain anything from beef stew to spaghetti and meatballs. They also come with a heater, which allows the recruits to warm up their food.

# Set to Graduate

During week nine, recruits who pass all parts of their training start preparing for BCT graduation. They take care of last minute details such as cleaning their barracks and getting fitted for their new uniforms.

At their graduation ceremony, platoons march together for family and friends who attend the event. By marching at the same pace, a platoon shows how it has learned to work together as a team. The recruits are now officially soldiers in the U.S. Army.

**Recruits during graduation from BCT**

A soldier's education does not end after BCT, however. Soldiers move on to advanced training for army jobs of their choice. Ian Fisher, for example, trained for a special combat team that eventually went to fight in Iraq, thus fulfilling his longtime dream. Like Ian, soldiers may be sent anywhere once they graduate. At home and overseas, they serve their country as part of the best fighting force in the world—the U.S. Army.

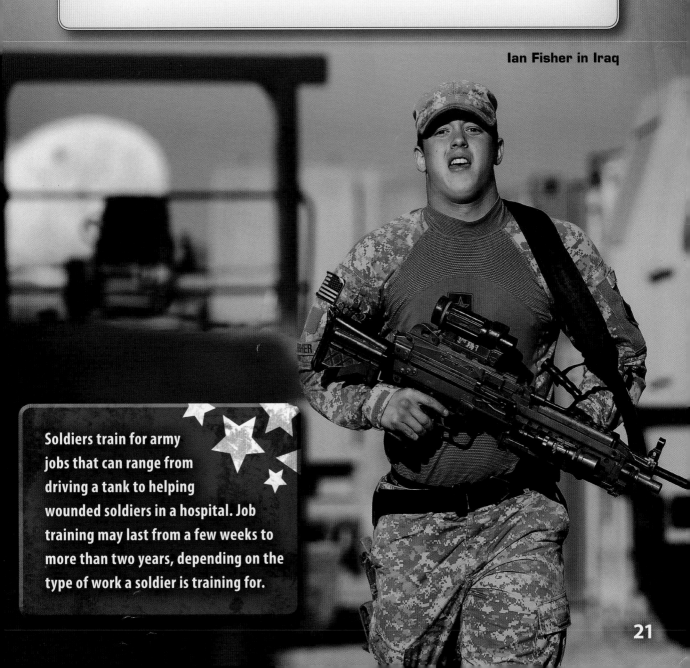

Ian Fisher in Iraq

Soldiers train for army jobs that can range from driving a tank to helping wounded soldiers in a hospital. Job training may last from a few weeks to more than two years, depending on the type of work a soldier is training for.

# Preparing for the Army

If you are interested in joining the army in the future, you can start preparing now by doing well in school, keeping your body in top physical shape, and being a responsible person. According to the U.S. government, the following rules apply:

★ You must be between 17 and 35 years old. If you are 17, you need your parents' permission to enlist.

★ You must be a citizen of the United States, or be a legal **immigrant** who is approved to live in the United States permanently.

★ You should have at least a high school diploma or a general **equivalency** diploma (GED). In some cases, the army will accept a person without a high school diploma or GED.

★ You must have no serious criminal record.

★ You must pass an army job skills test and a physical exam.

★ Before enlisting, you must decide on an army job to take up after you complete basic training. You can discuss your choices with an army official in your area.

# Glossary

**armed forces** (ARMD FORSS-iz) the military groups a country uses to protect itself; in the United States these are the Army, the Navy, the Air Force, the Marines, and the Coast Guard

**barracks** (BA-ruhks) the building or buildings where soldiers live

**bayonet** (BAY-uh-net) a long knife that's fastened to the end of a rifle

**civilians** (si-VIL-yuhnz) people who are not members of the armed forces

**combat** (KOM-bat) fighting between people or armies

**compass** (KUHM-puhss) an instrument used to find directions

**drill** (DRIL) an exercise or activity that is practiced over and over

**drill sergeant** (DRIL SAR-juhnt) an army officer who leads a group of recruits through basic combat training

**duffel bags** (DUF-ul BAGZ) long cloth bags that hold a soldier's clothing and equipment

**enlisted** (en-LIST-id) joined a branch of the armed forces

**equivalency** (i-KWIV-uh-luhn-see) being equal in value or significance

**grenade** (gruh-NADE) a small bomb that is thrown by hand

**immigrant** (IM-uh-gruhnt) a person who comes from one country to live permanently in a new one

**obstacle course** (OB-stuh-kuhl KORSS) a training course that is filled with hurdles, fences, and walls that soldiers must get over

**orientation** (or-ee-uhn-TAY-shuhn) a period of time spent learning about or getting used to something

**patriotic** (*pay*-tree-AH-tik) loving one's country and being ready to fight to defend it

**physical** (FIZ-uh-kuhl) having to do with the body

**platoon** (pluh-TOON) a group of soldiers who live and train together

**recruits** (ri-KROOTS) people who have recently joined the armed forces

**weapon** (WEP-uhn) something used in a fight to attack or defend, such as a knife, rifle, or bomb

# Index

# Bibliography

**Fritz, Sheila J.** *Behind the Spoon: Army Basic Training*. New York: Vantage Press (2007).

**Rice, Earle, Jr.** *The U.S. Army and Military Careers*. Berkeley Heights, NJ: Enslow (2007).

# Read More

**David, Jack.** *United States Army*. Minneapolis, MN: Bellwether (2008).

**Sandler, Michael.** *Army Rangers in Action*. New York: Bearport Publishing (2008).

# Learn More Online

To learn more about the U.S. Army, visit
**www.bearportpublishing.com/BecomingaSoldier**

# About the Author

Meish Goldish has written more than 200 books for children.
He lives in Brooklyn, New York.